Healing/Heeling

Sassafras Lowrey

For the dogs.

"I am perfectly aware that for people who do not love dogs, there will be too much about them in this story of John's life; but it is her life I am writing and not theirs, and to her, from childhood onwards, dogs were always an integral part of existence"
-Una Troubridge on Radclyffe Hall

(From "The Life and Death of Radclyff Hall" by Una Troubridge)

```
*




                              *
                          *.              *




                              *                        *




                                      *




                          *           *




              *
          *



      *


the dog star is and always will be the brightest light in the
                    night sky.
dogs are and always have been the light of my life
```

INTRODUCTION

I hold dog leashes the way that my grandmother clutched at rosary beads. Dogs have always made more sense to me than people. There is an old dog saying, "I want to be the person my dog thinks I am." These are not just words I live by, but a concept, a framework, a commitment, a dream, a goal. My life purpose is to live a life where I am worthy of the way my dogs look at me.

I have no idea what my first word/world was, but I wouldn't be surprised if it was dog. I've been magnetically and obsessively pulled to them my entire life: a passion that I cannot explain. Dogs are the part of my childhood I remember the most clearly, the brightness amidst fear and abuse. Dogs are what saved me again and again.

This collection is reflections of the dogs that broke me, alongside the stories of dogs who have made and saved me. In the beginning, I was raised by wolves. Ok not wolves, I was raised by a pack of dogs...small dogs. I told them my stories, the ones I couldn't write down. My stories were guarded by an angry rescued Lhasa Apso, one of the oldest types of dog, originally bred in Tibet- the job of these little lion dogs was to guard the monasteries. This small dog's job was to guard me, hard work in the home where I was raised. As a teenager, a terrier inspired the tenacity it took to run away, to dream/write a different life into existence. At the same time, a Shetland Sheepdog herded my stories to a safe place until I was able to write them down. Dogs have always found a way to protect and understand me. Dogs have broken my heart, leaving me emotionally incapacitated, and (other) dogs have brought me back to myself, back to dogs.

This is a collection of stories about dogs, and also of dog training, of obscure dog sports, a dance between dog and handler that through hybrid forms I have tried to bring to life on the page. This is also a book about queerness, my own identity(ies) and the community(ies) that I have found home and solace in. Queerness and dogs I have found go hand in hand, not only in my own trauma, but also in joy, companionship, and alternative family structures. My favorite stories have always been the ones about dogs, the dogs that find us, save us, know us better than anyone else.

When I was in elementary school, Lassie was my hero. I dreamed that she would come to save me. I carried a stuffed animal that resembled her everywhere. I talk about dogs constantly, more than people at dinner parties and literary events would probably like. I can't help it. I wouldn't want it any other way. Though dogs often find their way into my fiction, and I regularly write health, training and behavior articles for dog magazines there are other stories that I haven't written about, until now. I am thrilled to finally have this opportunity to bring my dog stories together in one place.

Sassafras Lowrey

January 2019

AGILITYGIRL2002

In high school, late at night my friends, dog girls mostly from California and I would chat on AOL. We had met online in agility discussion board and as the only teenagers developed a friendship. All night we talked about our dogs. We knew almost nothing about each other's lives beyond the shared passion for training and competing in agility (and other dog sports). Dog people don't care about people. It wasn't relevant I was being abused, I never asked if people made fun of them in school. Instead we perfected using keyboard symbols to create agility courses.....

|---| - jump
()))))(((() - tunnel
/_/\ - Aframe
|==| - double jump
|O| - tire
{}---{} - wing jump
()))))///////////// - chute

A few years ago, a friend digitized and salvaged video from a disintegrating VHS tape that had survived my running away, being stored in a barn, then move after move after move since the day I was kicked out. I'm watching ghosts. The ghost of him, his black terrier body flying. The ghost of who I was. Who we were to each other.

I don't let myself try to date that show, don't let myself count how many days/weeks/months we would have together after that day before being ripped apart. I never would have imagined. I never could have believed that day running, qualifying a clean run. "Run fast, run clean." That in a few short months we would be separated.

0\\\\\>>>>>>

((0)))))))))))((((((((((0

                                               |-----|

                |-----|

|-----|

                            |-----|

              |-----|

|-----|

        0))))))))))))((((((((((0

                                 |-----|

For a while when I was homeless, couch surfing, the only thing that got me through a day was a desire to make my dogs proud – even though they weren't my dogs anymore. Even though they would never know. I couldn't let losing them have been for nothing.

START

Dog and handler cross the start line together, running. Dog on handler's left side. Directly into the **chute** a barrel with cloth attached[1]

Jump

Jump

Jump

Curve to the right and jump

Turn to the right and jump dog is now on the handler's left side

Sharp turn to the left, dog and handler run parallel to the plane of the jump

Jump

Jump

---

[1] Which now in 2018 is no longer a legal obstacle because of the dangers associated with it but was legal and common in 2001. It was also Snicker's favorite obstacle

I loved dog women who would never consider themselves to be feminists. I've only just realized I'm now the same age as those women were back then, mid-30s and me at seventeen. Our round bodies next to lean dogs. There is a Garth Brooks song about "that summer" a country boy, an older widowed woman with hands of leather and velvet. It's a story of desire, longing, questionable consent and at seventeen it was my favorite song.

That summer, when I didn't need sleep, the summer weeks before running away I stayed up all night, two chat windows open on my teal iMac. Phone cord tangled stretch from my mother's room to mine. One window AOL chats with agility girls, another, older lesbians in gay chat rooms. Every night

A/S/L[2]

"How do you know you are gay?" I asked in the gay honkytonk chat room after my dog friends had logged off.

Dog lands and pulls with handler towards the right

Jump

Enters into an open **tunnel** curved. Handler makes a front cross spinning facing the dog coming out of the **tunnel** to put the dog back on the right side

Dog exits the tunnel Jump

---

[2] Age/Sex/Location

Jump

That summer painting dog agility equipment. Earning free training classes for my dogs. Too tight sports bra, baggy t-shirts with dog graphics, oversized shorts, hair pulled back into a utilitarian ponytail.

Jump

Dog enters into another open tunnel that is curved

Jump

I longed to be the boyi in that song. I loved all these women, wanted to build a life with them. For the first time I felt like I had found people who liked me, who I was enough for. I tucked myself into bed each night beneath a dog breed quilt Becca had made for me for Christmas. Gifted to me on a cold night in the front seat of her van, breath fogging after we left barn practice with our dogs.

Jump

"you can't be a lesbian, you like male country singers best" she said as she flipped through my CD binder library another night at a gas station, driving south to Medford where we would spend the weekend, competing at a dog show. Separate beds. Small hotel room.

FINISH

HEALING/HEELING

START
　　FINISH

                                        HALT Sit

Send Over Jump
Handler Passes By |----| Send to
Jump

Left Turn
Dog Circles
Right
Left Turn Forward   HALT
Forward

Start.
Dog heels at handler's left side, normal pace, forward.

her jowled head tips up towards me
lips flap back
tongue dangling
withers at my thigh
cheese sweats my hand
together
we dance this new dance

Dog heels at handler's left side, takes jump remains in heel forward. Normal pace.

at seventeen
i walked onto a dirt arena in a rural Washington fairground
sat my dog at the start line and ran. |---| |---|
        |---| ()))))))))))))))))))))))
for the last time
over and through a rainbow of wooden obstacles
the kind I spent the previous summer painting with sand
coats to earn money for training
before I ran away
with my dogs
to live with my coach, who I was in love with
"you're over that gay thing, right?"
pleading voice, the first night I stayed with her
then, I became homeless
journal read
called to the office of my high school
told to never come home
the dogs who had licked away a childhood of bruises
were gone

Handler turns left 90 degrees, dog circles 360 degrees around handler to the right. Forward heel normal pace.

God is Dog spelled backwards
                                              I'm dyslexic

Halt. dog sits in heel. Handler and dog turn left 90 degrees. Heel forward. Normal pace.

"i could have missed the pain, but I'd of had to miss the dance" Is tattooed in decade old blurring cursive on my

calf surrounding a course map for a (different) dog sport
the one we ran in that Washington fairground.

```
        /_/\                        * * * * *
    |---|

()))))((((()                        |---|
```

inky paw prints blur my bicep
i carry
the loss of these dogs everywhere
i want to say my first word was
Dog
that might be a fantasy a lie
my mother was always too drunk to remember and I was
too afraid to ask
when I was small before there were real dogs
to escape the dark corners of my childhood
 i carried a stuffed collie with me everywhere
                        Dogs are in my blood.

**Dog sent away from handler over jump, handler
remains behind the plane of the jump, calling dog
around jump after landing. Dog circles behind
handler to return to heel.**

Rumi said:
"The wound is the place where the light enters you"

**Heel forward, normal pace. Dog and handler halt.
Dog sits in heel position.**

i heal with the dogs who teach me to trust (again)
my greatest passion
my biggest anxiety.

i wake with the worry my life could

<---

D   N   I   W   E   R

(rewind)

Dog and handler heel at normal pace through finish sign.

heeling at my side
healing me

STILL WITH ME

I went to church in the morning, snuck to the bathroom during giving peace. Since kindergarten when I was allowed to leave the church sanctuary alone I started to measure the service around how many times I could walk slowly past the Sunday school offices to the bathroom and wait, picking at the itchy edge of my pink lace dress, hiking up the sagging crotch of my opaque white tights. After church I ate doughnut holes – glazed were best, cake was tolerable. I hid behind my parent's legs. My parents weren't safe people, but they were a danger I knew. Strangers could be anything.

Since I was three years old, every birthday, every time I sat on Santa's knee, every night when the stars broke through Oregon clouds, I wished for one thing. **A DOG.** My room was full of stuffed ones, and picture books, and encyclopedias of dog breeds that I couldn't yet read but would page through as a bedtime story with a flashlight under the covers. The only thing I wanted in life was a dog, and every holiday, every birthday, my mother and stepfather said no. My mother had given away her basset hound after I'd been born. She didn't want a dog. They tried to convince me I didn't want a dog. It never worked. After church, we went home and changed. I pulled weeds while my step father mowed the lawn, before announcing we were going "for a drive."

"For a drive" was code for spending the next several hours in the car going……boring places like swap meets, or logging roads which sometimes ended in sparkling lakes but usually deadended in clearcuts. Other times it was scouting dilapidated neighborhoods for new rental houses. They'd told me we were going to look at another house he was thinking of buying. He was always buying worn out houses in rundown towns. We stopped at a small house not far from one of his rental properties, the ones I spent weekends and summer vacations painting for crumpled dollar bills and the promise of Happy Meals. My parents turned to face me, smiling. It was rare they were

happy so close to one another.

There's a dog inside this house.

And two little girls.

They are mean to the dog.

They pull his tail.

And ears.

He's afraid.

I met their parents last week.

They don't want the dog.

We thought

It was time to let you

GET A DOG!

I was in shock

I don't think I even said anything

He's a Lhasa Apso

I couldn't believe my mother knew a dog breed

His name is Peepers

I'll probably change his name

(I didn't)

The house was loud. I don't remember the family, just the noise – screaming children fighting over Barbies, a TV blaring, smoke, the smell of dog pee. But there he was, a matted blond mass huddled under a kitchen chair as far away from the chaos of the living room as he could get. When I had dreamed every night of a dog this was not exactly what I had pictured and yet I instantly contorted every dog fantasy: frisbee, sled dogs, Rough Collies saving lost children into this raggedy small dog. He was, thank goD, the answer to my prayers.

Peepers was not an easy dog to live with. He exemplified everything that is culturally disliked about small dogs. He could be nippy. He was always barky. He was distrustful of strangers and upon deciding they were friends would spend the rest of the visit humping their legs. Peepers was never fully potty trained. His preferred place to pee was the "oriental rug" from Costco that my mother laid on top of the wall to wall carpeting in the living room because she thought it looked cosmopolitan.

Peepers was my dream come true, but his life was also not always easy. The violence, and substance use and anger in my childhood home was not infrequently redirected onto him. I had few friends, at school, when my peers would write notes to pass to one another, I wrote letters to him. I would bring them home and read the notes asking about what his day had been like (locked outside on a deck), describing the loneliness of mine. The first time my mother was arrested, the time my step father threw a cookie jar at her, and threw her down stairs. My mother scratched my step father's face to **get him off of her.** She called the cops but he had marks so she left in the back of a police car. The police never asked me what happened. Peepers was barking and my step-father kicked him into a wall. I grabbed him, and my mother's purse and ran across

the street to a neighbor's house. That summer before I
started middle school, my mother and I lived in a hotel.
Peepers had to stay at my grandparent's house, where I
would visit him everyday and promise that we would be
back together.

Peepers died my sophomore year in high school. His
health had deteriorated and he was struggling to recognize
people. I spent as much time away from the house as I
could at dog shows and training with my younger dog
because being around my mother had become more
unpredictable, more drunk, more violent. I hate that I
didn't spend more time with him those final years, that I
spent so much time with my younger dog, escaping.

I (still) not able to forgive the moments I (have) fail(ed)
dogs.

Sometimes I think I should have brought some of Peepers'
ashes to the Oregon coast, a place he did find some joy on

the occasional family vacation. I've never been able to release those ashes anywhere because I think the only place he would have wanted to be was with me. But maybe that's just me being selfish. Still, after all these years. Peepers didn't have a large life, didn't go many places. I bring his memory with me everywhere. The day I ran away from my mother's home, I carried his ashes with me in a small wooden box.

He's still with me.

LOYAL

When I was in the second grade I ran for student council. A popularity contest. I was not a popular kid. I don't know why I decided to run. I was shy, anxious about speaking not just in public, but to anyone/everyone. I suspect a teacher suggested I run. I was very good at doing things I thought teachers wanted, things that would make adults happy. I would do anything to make them like me, since none of my classmates did.

To run for student council, to represent the class we had to give a speech. I said that I couldn't promise pizza for lunch every day, or longer recess (platforms the other candidate ran on) because that wasn't something that the student council had control over. I told my class I could give them something better. At this moment I pushed my brown suede headband from the top of my head to around my neck like a collar. I told them that I would be loyal, like a dog.

I was not elected to the student council.

BORN AGAIN

|---| |---| |===|
                         ()))))(((((((()

|O|

Send dog through tire jump with dog on handler's left side

Eventually I was the one to kick my step father out of the house. Through my childhood, he would leave on his own for weeks at a time, usually after a fight. After days or weeks my mother would ask him to come home. Or he would just appear one night automatic garage door announcing his arrival

Dog and handler turn slightly to the right dog takes jump

The night I kicked him out, he had my mother's jewelry box in his hand. She was huddled on the floor drunk. I told him to leave. I told him my dog trainer (who I spent all my free time with, including weekends camping at dog shows together in her trailer, and who I was definitely in love with) knew *EVERYTHING*. I emphasized that last word.

Dog remains on handler's right side and takes jump

A year later, I left too. Without my step father to fight with, my mom's drinking got worse and her anger was all directed at me. I took it as long as I could. I spent every weekend at dog shows or training, one night a week in the barn.

Dog on handler's right side takes the double jump

My coach told me she couldn't ignore the bruises anymore. I didn't want her to. I'd been intentionally letting her see them. I'd been telling. All the secrets about what happened in our house.

I ran away to the dog show the way other kids fantasize about joining the circus. When I lost that, when I lost my dogs, I didn't know if there was a place in the world for me. I felt as though my citizenship to the world of dogs had been revoked.

Before takeoff from the double jump, handler cues the tunnel dog takes tunnel.

For years, even though I shared my home with dogs, I stayed away from the world of dog. Finding queers, discovering the queer edges of the dog world, building my way back to training, sports, and working with dogs felt like rebirth.

0))))))))))))))))))))))))))))) |==| |---| |---| |0|

|---| |---| |---|

0)))))))))))((((((((((0

MY GREATEST FAILURE

The biggest regret of my life is the temporary foster/adoption of a border collie mix in Jacksonville Florida. I met my ex boifriend at a queer youth conference. Hy broke up with hys wife to start a relationship with me. I went to visit hym for two weeks, but didn't get back on my flight home to Portland, forfeiting the tickets. A gesture that at the time felt romantic.

We moved in with hys (homophobic and transphobic) grandmother, mother and sister- who had a horse at a barn that bordered on Klan territory, where we weren't allowed to hold hands or they would start shooting. We needed our own place. The best we could do was a roach infested second story apartment with doors that didn't lock, so we had to push a dresser in front of them every night. The apartment was conveniently located in a neighborhood

where the busses stopped running at 6pm every night. I
didn't drive.

At the pet shop I saw a handwritten sign "FREE DOG"
with a blurry photograph of a dog that looked like it
should be herding sheep on a grassy hillside or scaling a
rainbow of agility equipment. My ex had never had a dog.
Hy didn't want a dog. Hy didn't want me. Yet, hy agreed
hastily to the idea of meeting her, adopting her, so long as
I was paying. I paid for everything. I think hy was excited
by the idea that I would have something (other than hym),
that it would make sneaking away to continue hys
relationship with hys (ex) wife easier. I called the number
and twenty minutes later the foster mother handed me
Sydney's leash.

 "we thought we might keep her"

she'd said, "but you have so much dog experience, and
seem so nice."

Her husband nodded.

No one in Jacksonville had ever said I was nice.

We'd just gone grocery shopping, so I spent the rest of the money I had for the month on supplies for Sydney. My boifriend didn't understand why I wouldn't buy her food at Walmart where all of our meals came from.

"She deserves better than this"

                                        "better than

                        me"

I said forking a plastic cheese single into my mouth.

The first night with her home, my boifriend went out, leaving me and Sydney alone in the apartment. It was the first time I'd ever been alone there. No books, no television, no radio, a flip phone, friends three time zones away, some broken furniture we'd taken from hys mom's garage, me and this dog. I narrated to Sydney everything I did:

pushing the dresser in front of the door after my boifriend

left

washing the plastic dishes that filled the sink

killing a cockroach

hanging a shower curtain

 taking a shower

I took a picture of Sydney laying on the bed with a disposable camera that had a few pictures left.

In the morning, when my boifriend came home, neck dalmation spotted with hickies from hys (ex)wife, hy told me it was over, that hy was moving out, that hy didn't want to be with me anymore. Although hy was the first "serious" relationship I'd ever been in, I had suspected I was losing hym. I cried into Sydney's neck and took her outside to potty where strange men leered at me threateningly.

I knew I couldn't stay in Jacksonville if that relationship ended. I couldn't drive. I couldn't stay in that apartment. I had to go back to Portland. I called every airline that flew out of Jacksonville but none could fly a dog in the summer. I called the train companies, the bus companies and none could accept a dog. I dreamt about the times my dog trainer had tried to teach me how to drive (before kicking me out). I'd had panic attacks driving her van down the gravel driveway and refused to continue. If I had learned to drive, I could have saved Sydney.

The summer before, I had been getting ready to start my senior year in high school, not yet having runaway, not yet becoming homeless. I never could have pictured where I would be a year later. For a day, I fantasized that I was still that girl with the long brown hair from the summer before: with dog connections and friends, that I could find a way to travel across the country with Sydney from dog show to dog show, giving people gas money, working as a kennel hand. In the mirror of the queer community center where I went to use the internet I saw myself: short blue hair, piercings, I was trapped. I had no allies in the dog world anymore. There was no way to get her home.

The day I handed Sydney's leash back to the foster parents, in the same pet store parking lot they told me they had missed her terribly and would never send her away again. I hope that's true. My ex drove me to give Sydney back. I handed her parents everything I'd bought for her. I wouldn't accept their money. Sydney deserved a stable family, more stability than I was able to give her. That night, and every night for months after I dreamed of leash after leash being ripped from my fingers. I felt like I had failed everything.

All I have are four photographs of her on a cracked tile floor of that apartment, and on a celestial blanket that was the bed she and I slept together on. Sydney was only in my life for seventy two hours, but I have never forgotten how helpless I felt when I couldn't save her. Days after I lost her before I left Jacksonville, I tattooed a pawprint for her on my arm that I look at every day, as a reminder of my failure. I have never forgiven myself for not being able to keep her.

I have never written this story before.

BEGIN. AGAIN.

|------| ()))))))))))))))))))))))))))))))))

                                    |-------|

              |-------|

Dog begins on handler's right side facing handler. Handler pulls hand back slightly turning the dog's head to the right to wrap them and now be facing the jump. Dog goes over jump, handler turns to the right and runs towards the tunnel, dog follows handler without back jumping.

I found dog sports again because of the queer performance artist Holly Hughes. I didn't know her then, but attended her one woman show *The Dog & Pony Show* at Dixon Place in New York City.

"It's about dogs" my partner had said – convincing me to leave Brooklyn, our cozy apartment and dogs, and go to Manhattan for experimental performance art.

Dog goes through tunnel, handler remains behind

Holly was the first out queer person I'd met who trained or competed in dog sports.
She was the first person I'd met in over a decade who understood the language of dog.

I cried during her performance.
I couldn't breath.
I had forgotten what it felt like to have a shared
(dog)language.
I'd never even hoped to find it with another queer person.

"I need to meet her" I whispered to my partner during the
curtain call in the black box theater.

**Dog exits tunnel and turns sharply to the right as
handler calls dog over jump**

I don't talk to people, but I wouldn't allow myself to leave
the theater without approaching Holly.

I don't know what I said amidst sputtering words
When I was
                                        High school
                    Junior Handler
                        Queer
                                                Dogs
                    Loss
Homeless
                        Dogs
                                            Agility
Dogs
Dogs
Dogs

**Handler backs up towards the next jump facing the
dog who is running towards them. Dog comes into
handler's right hand next to the jump bringing the
dog right next to the jump standard before turning
their head to the right and sending the dog over the
jump.**

At some point I stopped stuttering, turned around and
showed Holly the agility course map tattooed on my calf.


```
                    0)))))))))((((((((((0


          | 0 |


                        /***********************\


    | --- |                           | ----- |



                | ---- |


       | ---- |
```

**Dog and handler begin with dog on the handers left
side. Dog crosses over Jump**

I don't remember what Holly said, but I know she hugged
me. She pulled her partner over, and showed her my
tattoo. She gave me her phone number and said we needed
to have lunch together before she left town.

**Dog and handler turn slightly to the right, dog takes
Jump**

I clutched the paper
we scheduled lunch for later in the week.

Dog and handler turn slightly to the right dog takes Jump

She said there were others, dog people, queer dog people
and offered to introduce me to them.

Dog moves forward at speed through Tire jump

I remembered seventeen
Rural Washington
Dirt
Fairgrounds

Purple hair
Rainbow tshirt
Dykes
Closeted
Living and training together
"Just friends"
They said
Refused to make eye contact with me
The day before she kicked me out
The day before
I lost my dogs
I kept trying to meet their eyes

Dog goes into tunnel, handler remains on left side

()))))))))(((((()

|---|

|---|

Dog enters tunnel on handler's left side

Holly introduced me to a trainer she'd known for decades,
a queer dyke who competed at the levels of agility that I'd
only dreamed about.
 I'd read training articles written by her when I was a junior
handler

Dog exits tunnel and moves towards jump

She offered to let me become her assistant for her NYC
classes
 I had a panic attack

                                                But said yes

**Handler gets ahead of dog while dog is in the tunnel
to setup a front cross. Handler pivots in front of jump,
keeping eye contact and connection with dog.
 Handers pivot ends with them on the dog's right
side, on the right side of the jump**

We became family through her blue border collie, my
goddaughter. Week by week I watched as she helped
beginners fall in love with the sport that had changed the
course of my life. I learned there were more LGBTQ folks

in the dog world than closeted teenage me could have ever fantasized.

Unsurprisingly many continue to remain closeted due to the conservative nature of the dog world.

She had me guest teach her classes.

She vouched for me to get a puppy.

Dog orients from handler's cross and takes the next jump which is at an angle from the previous jump. Handler on right.

Recapturing stolen dreams

COURSE MAP

Start   Finish

                                                   HALT Sit

Send Over Jump
Handler Passes By   I——I   Send to Jump

Left Turn   HALT
Dog Circles Right   Left Turn
Forward   Forward

Start.
Dog heels at handler's left side, normal pace, forward.

12 months ago your eyes weren't yet open
I was praying to every first star in the sky for you
Now you sparkle
Now you prance
In every class
In every sport
We play
We dance this new dance

Dog heels at handler's left side, takes jump remains in heel forward. Normal pace.

16 years ago
was the last time I walked into a ring with a dog
before they were ripped from my side.
this sport barely existed, I love that it's something new that we can learn
Together.
I think of those dogs that were stolen from me every day.
I believe all these years later, they watch over me
Always

Handler turns left 90 degrees, dog circles 360 degrees around handler to the right. Forward heel normal pace.

"I could have missed the pain, but I'd of had to miss the dance" Is tattooed in blurring cursive on my calf.
surrounding a course map for a (different) dog sport.
dog portraits on my arms and legs

Black inky paw prints blurry on my bicep for each of you
dogs are in my blood.

**Halt. dog sits in heel. Handler and dog turn left 90
degrees. Heel forward. Normal pace.**

I heal a little more through this new dance
through you being at my side
I heal with the dogs who have taught me to learn to
trust
again

**Dog sent away from handler over jump, handler
remains behind the plane of the jump, calling dog
around jump after landing. Dog circles behind
handler to return to heel.**

you have letters after your name
titles we've earned
CGC
TDCH
TKP
but what matters far more is that we've done it together
your joyful prance
your drive to work
at my side.
the way you chose me
on that deck in New Jersey last winter when I met your
litter
I'd prayed that morning to my lost dogs to guide me to the
right
puppy

**Heel forward, normal pace. Dog and handler halt.
Dog sits in heel position.**

Dogs heal me in ways nothing else can

my greatest passion
my biggest anxiety.
everyday I worry my life could
rewind
that I could relive my worst day
losing
my dogs
the best medicine to heal me
my best friends
my family
my greatest source of panic.
someday I hope the nightmares stop
that I won't keep reliving losing them
That I won't wake fearing losing you

Dog and handler heel at normal pace through finish sign.

Dogs make more sense to me than people.
good girl
pretty baby
all the cheese for
you
thank you for choosing
me
for choosing
this
for choosing
us.
for heeling at my side
for healing me

RALLY CLASS

START

Serpentine
Weave Once

*

HALT Step in Front
Finish Right- Forward

*
*

     *

        *

*

HALT   Spiral Left - Dog Inside
Call Front
Finish Right

Moving Side Step Right

About Turn
Right

FINISH

* = cones

Dog and handler begin the exercise side by side.

She heels at my left side, head even with the seam of the jeans I don't wear. I remember when I began competing in dog sports. I was a tomboy. It was an excuse to be devantly gendered. A solidarity amongst these dog women, until I pushed too far. Until I came out. Until I was not just a sloppy woman, I was queerly desiring, sexual in my baggy shirts and ill fitted jeans.

Now, in my return to dog sports, my queered femininity, my refusal to dress down makes me conspicuous. My queerness marked

Dog and handler approach four orange cones. The dog still heeling at the handler's left side weave in and out of the cones in a serpentine pattern with the dog closest to the cones, entering the serpentine between the first and second cone.

"Are you sure your dog can work if you're wearing a skirt?"
I laugh
If my dogs couldn't heel with me in a dress
They never would

Dog and handler stop. Dog automatically sits at the handler's left side. The handler calls the dog to front position, where the dog gets up, comes to face the handler and sit, in front of them looking into their face. The dog is released to then go around the handler's right side to return to the left side heel position and sit.

Sixteen years ago tonight I was locked out of the trailer I was staying in at a dog show because my coach who had taken me in had just read my journal and discovered I was a lesbian. She was angry. My dogs and I walked around the fairgrounds in the dark, looking at the yellow glow through each trailer window. A winter trial, there were no tent campers, no outside grillers. Everyone was inside. We walked until finally she called my name and we were allowed back in. She told me it was time for bed. My dogs and I slept in a sleeping bag on one side of the trailer, her on the other, silent. In the morning she changed clothes in the travel trailer's tiny bathroom with the door locked.

The dog and handler heel forward together.

I don't know who i am without dogs.

The dog and handler make a right turn in unison, to cue move silently to the dog the handler slows, slightly exaggerates the step with the left foot, closest to the dog and they continue on together.

While heeling forward the handler takes a large exaggerated step to the right, the dog side steps to join the handler, and they continue heeling forward.

Sixteen years ago, I got paged to the office of my high school to take a call from my dog agility trainer who I was living with. I was 17. The day after we got home from the trial where she locked me outside, she read my whole journal. She knew I was queer. She told me never to come "home" again. I lost my dogs. This was the hardest day of my life, but I had no idea what a beautiful queer world awaited me.

To the left are three cones, the middle cone is one of the four cones that had been part of the earlier serpentine. Dog and handler heeling with the dog

closest to the cones circle to the left the third cone, then the second, then the first in a pattern that if visible would resemble a paperclip, ending the exercise where they began.

Sixteen years ago I became homeless, and lost my dogs. The most traumatic thing that ever happened to me was the way they were taken from me. Last month I asked my partner if ze thought I would ever not panic, ever not fear I was losing my dogs. I will always live with this fear.

I'm back where I began, training dogs, playing with dog sports, my oldest passion. My biggest source of trauma.

Heeling forward dog at handler's left leg. Handler and dog stop, dog automatically sits at handler's left side, ear even with the (in my case nonexistent) handler's pants seam. Handler leaves and steps in front of their dog facing her. Handler then calls the dog to finish right, the dog moves towards the handler circling around the handler's right side to return to heel position on the handler's left side.

The entire (dog)world turned its back on me that day. Wouldn't take my calls, wouldn't help me keep my dogs.

Dog and handler then heel forward together at normal pace past the finish sign

Sixteen years ago I never could have imagined I'd have dogs again or be walking rally sequences while my partner took video.

Exercise finished.

FLASH

Flash made his competitive agility debut at twelve months old, nearly to the day. It was (then) the youngest he could legally step into the ring.

I lost Flash two months before his second birthday

Snickers played agility because he loved me
Flash just loved agility

I met him, a tri-colored wobbly fur ball on a picturesque green farm in Western Oregon.
I had been the top novice/open handler in my regional agility club the year before
I was a passionate and committed jr handler
Who competed with adults
I was looking for a puppy to keep up with my passion for the sport

Flash's favorite obstacle was the weave poles
He could weave before he could heel (back then we taught weaving early)
Weave poles are arguably the most difficult obstacle for dogs

| | | | | |

A dog weaving must slalom
Weave between six poles – or twelve, depending on the venue and level

| | | | | | | | | | | |

The dog must always enter the poles on the left – popping out, or needing to restart results in a penalty

Flash's registered name Flash On Contact[3]– following the kennel name. Flash was bred to play agility. Spooky and uncertain in the world, but you put a rainbow of obstacles in front of him and Flash could do anything.

He flew on every course with qualifying runs – run fast, run clean (no faults) his debut weekend in the ring.

Flash taught me to handle at speed.

When my trainer kicked me out she kept Flash.

"I don't care what you do with Snickers, but I want Flash." She told me on the crackling phone the day she called my high school and told me to never come back.

She threatened that if I rehomed him to anyone else she would contact his breeder, say the home was unfit and get him anyway.

Flash was full of potential.

Ten months after I lost him, head shaved, face pierced, (somewhat) stably housed, I got a ride to the County Fairgrounds: the dirt arenas where I had spent most of my teen years at trials.

```
/_/\            |---|                    |---|
   ())))))))))))))))))))))         |---|
```

---

[3] The yellow area at the end of contact obstacles where a dog must put at least one foot into before moving forward on the course.

It was the Halloween show. I hadn't seen my (ex) trainer since she took Flash's purple leash out of my hand, the day that I became homeless.

I hadn't planned to talk to her. I just wanted to see Flash, but he wasn't listed in the show catalogue

Where is Flash?

I confronted her when she finished walking a course – the private dance ritual where sans dogs handlers walk the obstacles in the order they will run them, memorizing it and planning how they will guide their dog. Courses are different each time. Dogs do not see the course until they leave the start line.

He has a faulty temperament

Too anxious in the trial setting

Retraining

Reevaluating

Not Here

I had given her Flash because I had no choice, because she engineered a situation where I was going to be homeless. I had believed that even if she hated me, hated my gayness, that her ambition would give Flash the kind of future I could no longer give to him, the kind of future that he deserved, training and competing in a sport he loved.

Occasionally, over the years, I have searched his registered name (a dog -world social security number). The only recorded Q's (qualifying runs that build together towards titles) are the title that I put on him.

In the end I have to live knowing that she lied.

ABOUT TURN

START

1.HALT
STAND
WALK AROUND

2.FIGURE 8 WITH DISTRACTION

*

<dog food bowl>   <dog food bowl>
    ()   ()

*

FINISH

3. HALT
4.HALT   TURNRIGHT,
STEP   CALL TO HEEL
LEFT TURN   HALT
FORWARD

5. ABOUT U TURN
FORWARD

* = cone

CHOOSE DOG

START

360° Right

FINISH

Normal
Pace

Call
Front
Finish Right
Forward

HALT
Fast Forward
From Sit

Loop Right

270° Left Turn

About Turn
Right Forward

BACKUP   ABOUT TURN
3 STEPS

START

STAND
LEAVE
DOWN
CALL TO FRONT
FINISH SIT

HALT
STEP IN FRONT
FINISH LEFT
FORWARD

CALL YOUR DOG

DOUBLE LEFT
ABOUT TURN

FINISH

Dog and handler begin heeling together with the dog at the handler's left side head even with the inseam.

Some people have a baby to save a relationship
I got a dog to ruin mine
18 years old
My second serious relationship
His collar around my wrist
Belt (consensually) to my back
I wanted our relationship to end
But couldn't admit it

**Dog and handler stop, and take three steps
backwards together.**

He stayed home and did drugs while I went to the animal
shelter
With my friend
His ex
the way of queer punk kids

**Dog and handler make a u-turn to the right and
continue walking together in heel position.**

**Handler and dog stop. Dog is left in a stand stay.
Handler walks to the next sign, stops, turns around to
face the dog, and asks the dog to down. Dog is
released from the down and called to the front
position sitting directly in front of the handler. Dog is
then asked to flip finish on the handler's left side
ending while seeing in heel position.**

Cosmo was a border collie
With an obsessive love of toys
Chasing my ex's cats
And me

Heel forward and then take a u turn, about turn to the right while the dog walks in heel.

My ex had never lived with dogs until he moved into my
life
He tolerated my chihuahua
And would grow to hate my collie

Dog and handler turn in a circle to the left twice together and then continue heeling.

He tried to convince me to abandon dogs
Said they were bad for me
That I loved them too much
That they distracted me from
Him

Dog and handler stop. Dog sits. Handler steps in front of dog. Dog flips into finish on the handler's left side. Dog and handler heel forward together. And exercise is finished.

I was young in love and leather
Believed him
Stopped buying dog magazines with my extra cash
Stopped training
Stopped dreaming
I could ever have dogs back
As my life

*

    *

       *

SPIRAL LEFT

               HALT RIGHT TURN

            SPIRAL LEFT
        HALT
CALL FRONT
       FINISH RIGHT
      FORWARD
            HALT SIT

180* RIGHT

            360* RIGHT

       FAST

NORMAL

   FINISH
       SLOW

       START

180* LEFT

START dog heels at handler's left side

Once we drove all night to Canada

And slept in the back of his beater car with the dogs

After border patrol interrogated us

Searched the car

My dogs

Border patrol didn't understand why we didn't know the

(Legal) name for the punks whose driveway we were to crash in

In the morning I crawled out into the foggy Vancounter dawn

Cosmo at my side

We played ball

In an empty park

Even then I knew he would leave me

I knew

I would always pick the dogs

Slow pace

The night we broke up he stayed out with his new boyfriend

I dreamt the breakup had already happened

When he came home and said it was over

I said

I know

And took my dogs for a walk

Fast pace

That night he asked to be alone at the apartment

Said he wanted to pack his things

Said he wanted to say goodbye to the dogs

I came home early the next morning to my dogs being gone

Dog and handler make a 180* right turn with dog in heel position

Trigger

Rewind

Panic

Calling

Punk house landlines

Leaving

Desperate messages

Until the tape ran out

Rewind

Panic

Rewind

Normal pace heeling

He brought the dogs home and I told him to never ask to see them again

He didn't

He cared for them even less than he had ever valued me

Dog and handler make 180* turn and heel forward at an angle

There is a faded photograph of Cosmo and Mercury in a bike trailer designed for toddlers that I bought from a family for $15 at a garage sale

Dog and handler stop, dog sits in heel position. Handler calls dog to move in front of them sitting with dog facing handler. Dog goes around behind

handler's right side and returns to left-side heel position sitting.

I became obsessed with the idea of transporting my dogs

Anywhere

Dog and handler spiral around three cones in the shape of a paper clip. Heeling around the third cone, then second cone, then last cone

Everywhere

Dog and handler stop, dog sits in heel position, then turn right

So we could never be separated

Dog and handler spiral to the left in a tight circle together in heel position

The dogs and I rented a basement room and lived there ten months. I the the longest we had been .... anywhere since I ran away

Dog and handler stop, dog sits in heel position

We moved a lot

Dog and handler spiral to the right in a tight circle together in heel position

Homophobic, transphobic, dogphobic landlords

FINISH

Fighting to stay together, searching for home.

SNICKERS

Snickers was my dream puppy. Born to the wannabe-backyard breeders of our neighborhood whose house was decorated with ivory, zebra skins and other illegal "souvenirs" stolen from Kenya and other countries where they had gone on mission trips. Their African Grey parrot who called the house's dogs and scolded them

They were the most exotic thing in our suburban neighborhood.

I borrowed the polaroid camera out of my step-father's closet and took a picture of a squirming 4 week old black fuzzy caterpillar the size of a candy bar. He had consistently crawled to me every afternoon when the neighborhood children converged on the little yellow house in the middle of the subdivision to visit the puppies.

I wrote a letter and left it on the steps for my step father to see when he came home from work. I made my "case" for why I should be allowed a puppy. I don't remember what I wrote – something about honor roll, about my dream for dog sports.

The only thing I ever asked for as a kid were dogs.

My step father (who tortured my mother and I) relented.

 "She is a good kid."

"She never asks for anything."

 I remember hearing him say my ear pressed to my bedroom door, listening, praying while they read my letter.

Snickers was mine.

He would sleep next to me every night. He would be my first teammate.

Snickers was an unlikely athlete, but he played with me, for me. Because it was something we did together, heeling in time to the click click click of the metronome. Tracking in dew of fields following the baby scent of dragged turkey legs.

He couldn't pass the CGC because he couldn't tolerate being away from me for the required five minutes and held by a stranger with me out of sight. I don't want to think about the decade he would go on to spend without me.

Together Snickers and I received the top novice beginner team award from our local agility club.The plaque is rotting in a landfill along with the dozens and dozens of ribbons and medals we earned.

FROM STREET DOG TO CHAMPION

Left Turn

Left Turn   Normal Pace   Slow Pace   Call Front/
                                         Finish Left

Double Serpentine   Sit/Down/Walkaround   Right
Turn

*
*
*
*
*
                360R   *

                                                  *

                                                  *
                                         Serpentine

                    FINISH

            START   Moving Sidestep 270R

62

Dog and handler heel together at normal pace. Dog and handler take moving sidestep to the right.

Fear feels like the collapse of the planet
Fear is the atmosphere closing in
You are my cosmic twin
We mask fear with bravado
Until we can't
Fear overtaking

Dog and handler circle 270 degrees to the right in heel position.

I don't know where you were born
This keeps me up at night
I don't talk about where I'm from

Serpentine

The dogcatcher found you
25 pounds on the bones of a 50 pound
Dog
Puppies suckling at your rib bones
The first picture
You
Wide eyed
The puppies you
Kept alive
Saved you
Masked your
Broken brain
Got you to
New York
We were brought together by
Angels

Left Turn

I got the letter from my grandmother that Snickers died
Bringing you in the front door
He brought you to me
The Merriam-Webster dictionary says binary stars are:
Noun:
"A system of two stars that revolve around each other
under their mutual gravitation."
We orbit together around
Fear

Call Front Finish Left

We are orbiting the same
Panic
The world spins
Yet you lead me forward
Back to the world of dogs
Back to a version of myself where I feel at home
I believe
The (lost) dogs of my past brought you and I
together

Slow Pace
Last year you broke three teeth
And cut your paw in panic
A freak thunderstorm approaching but not on the
Forecast
We live our life around forecasts
Me
10 minutes from
home
I couldn't get home fast enough

Normal Pace
You work so hard to do the things

Other dogs take for granted.
"I know what it's like to be so afraid you hurt yourself"
An old friend
Who I once shared a moldy punkhouse basement with
Says on Facebook when I talk about the storm
People like to focus on how challenging you are
How we needed to buy you a house
And then sold it
Moved cross country
They focus on
What you can't do
The way you need special care
Focus
Behavioral management
To give you the biggest world possible

Turn Left
They say you are lucky

Double Serpentine
They don't see the worlds you led me back to
You
Not my service dog
Yet my guide

Sit/Down/Walkaround
Back to the worlds I thought were torched
When I threw all the
Ribbons
Rosettes
Medals
Those dogs and I had
Won
Save one
Into the trash compactor of the
12th apartment in 14 months
Since I became

Homeless
Since I lost the
The dogs

Right Turn
You have guided me back
Together one trick at a time
One title
Then another
Complicated tricks
Reaching the highest level of the sport
Making you a champion
Ribbons almost bigger than you

360R
Some days I feel like my anxiety will
Crush me

Finish
You have those days too

GOODBYE NYC

City dogs roam the avenues in packs
Tethered
Leash clipped
Carabiners to
(often distracted) downtown actors
Underemployed professors
Punks
Artists

City dogs roam
In neat webbed mases
Down afternoon streets
While their parent(s)
Sit
In office board rooms
Dance on stages
Hide in cubicles

Urban packs draw phones from tourist pockets
There packs bring smiles
To the weary commuter faces
The dogless masses
And those whose own dogs are left behind
2, 3, 4, deadbolt locks

Pack of dogs begging for sidewalk game – hotdogs,
pretzels

Rain or shine these packs roam
City streets
Their parents satisfied with the knowing their dogs have
gone out, giving them permission to stay out past dog
parent curfews
Hitting happy hour
Dinner

A show
The dogs waiting behind
2, 3, 4 deadbolt locks

SERVICE DOG

When I was eighteen, newly (mostly) stably housed, the therapist I briefly saw suggested I should work with a service dog. Leaving my apartment had become almost impossible:
three locks
two hallways
four steps to the outside.
Four blocks to the bus
was a marathon I found myself gasping to complete. I was bound by panic, by the threat that anxiety could tackle me to the ground in the grocery store, at the bank, in school. Safer to stay inside, hidden my brain convinced me.

I am
Have always been
An emotional
Edgeplayer

It was perhaps a radical idea to use a dog to help me to heal from the trauma caused by losing the dogs.

High functioning (on a good day) anxiety, PTSD were the official diagnoses. I became room bound by my anxiety attacks. For stretches I couldn't leave my room, couldn't go to school, convinced I would rewind and find myself in that suburban bedroom
Dirty pink carpet
Hoarded hallways
Green glass wine bottles
Under every sink
In trash bags driven to the recycling center
Every weekend

My mother's acrylic nails
Washing me in the bathtub

Even in high school
She couldn't allow me to have
My own
Body

A high percentage of service dogs "wash out" – deemed
inappropriate for work, don't master the tasks, or the
public access.
I was lucky
Mercury didn't
Mercury worked
Harder than any dog
I've ever known
Giving me (my) life

I didn't think that I was worthy of being saved. I didn't
think I was worthy of Dog forgiving me for having failed
my dogs.

When his vest went on he knew he had a job. Overnight it
was possible for me to go to the grocery store, ride the
bus- even over bridges.

I was saved by a dog who weighed ten pounds. I went
back to college, made Dean's list instead of being on
academic probation. Mercury heeled at my side down
college hallway corridors, and settled me, laying at my feet
in lecture halls

Waiting

For me to need him – paws on my knees, jumping up,
scratching at my shins, digging digging digging me back
from dissociation. Nose to skin, alerting me. To tread
carefully, that panic could overtake me. Healing.

Dig

Dig
Digging
Me out of fear
Of the broken rewind of panic and trauma where I don't
recognize what's real or who I am

I owe my life to the smallest dog I have ever shared my
heart with
The dog who has been with me from near homelessness
 to homeowner
From lost to loved
Silenced to author
He moved with me through slumlords all the homophobic
neighbors. My priority was to give him stability which in
turn stabilized me. He has slept pressed against me
Heart to heart
For sixteen years

When he retired, it was because I was (mostly) healed. My
panic (usually) no longer daily debilitating, but even
without a vest, he watches over me in my sleep, my guard
dog protecting me from what comes for me in the
darkness, the tendrils of memory drifting closer

He sleeps
Always watching
Even now when vision has left his eyes
Waking me if
The nightmares sneak past his guard
The nightmares are always leash ripped from hand
screaming
This used to be our nightly routine
He and I didn't sleep too much back then

DOG HOUSE

I live in a dog house
By which I don't mean a four walled
Slanted roof
The kind I painted at seven
And begged my parents to never force my beloved dog
To sleep in
Though they did
On an upper deck
When I had to go to school

when you buy a house for a dog
when your family changes living arrangements
constructs
schedules
careers
around the needs of a dog
you become a
different
type of dog person

Charlotte's needs have dictated all aspects of our life.
When the co-op apartment we shared for eight years
arbitrarily enacted anti-dog policies, which conveniently
coincided with some shady financial decisions by the
board, we put our apartment on the market and bought
Charlotte a house.

I am not good at change, but if you come for my dogs, I
will change anything and everything. The co-op board, led
by a dog hating woman (who was afraid of my 10 pound
former service dog) decided: dogs should be muzzled in
public areas of the building.
Should never ride the elevator if anyone was present

Shouldn't bark, lean, pull, make any sounds in public areas
of the building
Were a risk
A nuisance
That if anyone was uncomfortable with a dog they could
request it be
Removed
From its home
And, finally, that all dogs had to be approved by the co-op
board, including dogs who had called the building home
longer than some co-op board members had owned their
apartments

Rewind
Panic

My nightmares were flooded with memories
Fear I would
Could
Lose my dogs
A key reason I'd wanted to buy in that building had been
The low key approach to dogs
So different from most NYC co-ops

For years, we had managed Charlotte's anxiety, her
triggers, her reactivity in a 101 unit building that took up
most of a city block. Where every walk involved an
elaborate dance criss crossing sidewalks and jaywalking to
avoid other dogs. She was tired. She deserved more so we
moved. The primary requirement of a new house was
quiet, and a yard to give Charlotte her own world

We put an offer on the house five minutes after leaving the
open house. The (small) yard was perfect because it would
be hers. The house ideal. I knew immediately it was to be
Charlotte's house

Yes, privilege.

I'm not unaware of how lucky we are to be able to give her a life like this.

I'll never forget the first time she came to the house, the morning after closing. It was lightly snowing. There was a soccer ball abandoned in the yard.

We don't share clear languages with dogs, but in that moment I knew she knew, that she understood this home was hers.

She RAN for the first time off leash in a place where she was safe

We were safe.

As I write, we are selling Charlotte's sanctuary house that still couldn't meet her needs.

Preparing to move 3000 miles to the state I am from

The place I lost those dogs

Lost a world

To give her a chance at a bigger life

Without thunder

Bigger yard

A quieter life

A world with fewer (of her) triggers

FEATHERS

I've begun seeing feathers again. It isn't that the angels
have left me – I know that the boys are always with me. I
am ready to tell their story.

 I don't remember when the feathers started following me.
I had cried myself to sleep looking at photographs.

"If you are there, give me a sign."

Give me a sign that you haven't left me forever
(Don't worry, I don't usually believe these things either but
                                        I believe in Dog)
Then the feathers began appearing: predictable places like
beaches and in parks, but also right in my path on bustling
sidewalks,and carpeted apartment hallways. Fluttering.

The feathers came with dreams
With signs
That the dogs I felt I failed had forgiven me
                                If only I could forgive myself.

Last night I dreamt an eagle feather, as long as my arm. It
was a message from all the dogs to me. Big. Bold. Right as
I woke so I couldn't forget
They are always with me.

dogs have never forsaken me, even when it felt like the
goD of my childhood, of patriarchy and brimstone had
left me.
Thank Dog
I have never
Been alone.

QUEER DOG PEOPLE PROBLEMS

WHEN SOME FRIENDS ARE AT A
BDSM PUP PLAY COMPETITION &
OTHERS ARE AT A MAJOR DOG
SHOW….SOCIAL MEDIA REQUIRES A
DOUBLE TAKE!

PANIC

0))))))))))))((((((((((0

|---|

|---|

|---|
                    |O|

0)))))))))((((((((((0

|---|

|---|

Dog and handler begin moving forward together with dog on handler's left. Jump

Dog and handler turn to the left, dog takes Jump

Dog and handler turn to the left, dog takes Jump

Dog jumps through Tire

Driving ahead of handler, dog takes Tunnel

()))))))))((((((((((O

|0|

|---| |-----|

|----|

Your world ends a little with each firework pop
Each clap of thunder
Applauding the destruction of the world

I know what panic feels like

Healing/Heeling

Sounds like
Smells like

Through taking care of your embodied panic, the
Shake and quake of your fear
I'm learning to be more comfortable talking about my own
The way the world falls away
Hands tremble
Heart racing
Joints freezing
As my mind a silent echo chamber plays scenes
Of every
Bad
Thing
That has ever happened
Leashes ripped from hands
Fists
Screams
My panic is
noise canceling headphones
trapping me in a repeat
repeat
repeat
repeat
repeat
repeat
repeat
repeat
until you bring me back
paw on skin
wet
cold
nose
on face
fingers clench fur

DREAM VISITS

Of all the dogs I've known and lost
The one who
was the spookiest,
The flightiest
Is Flash
He came to me
In my dreams
Tonight I awoke in an
Iowa truck stop
feeling the presence of him, the flirt of his white tipped tail
Dashing through my mind herding me toward dream and
away from nightmare

The dogs of my past are always with me
I carry my canine ancestors as
Guides
Flash visits me so seldom as I awoke I reached for my
phone to write these memories of seeing Him
I see the signs of their presence in the feathers
They send hints to me, proof from their angel wings that
they are with me
Always

Flash was the spookiest dog I've had
Until now
Well bred
Well trained
He shouldn't have been
But he was
She shouldn't be
But she is
My twenty month old Newfoundland who is
The largest dog I've ever shared my life with
And easily as afraid of noises, strangers appearing, oddly
shaped pieces of metal as Flash was

I regret I have never had the chance to bring Flash to
sheep
To see the kind of work he would
have loved, the work he was bred to do
If given the opportunity

There is
A certain magic to me in watching a dog
Do the work that they were bred to do
Flash was happiest when working
The first time he stepped into an agility ring
He qualified, completing the course fast and without faults.
It had taken me many months of trials with Snickers to
achieve the same (slower but clean) results
Different dogs
I was a better handler with my second dog
But also
Flash loves the game in ways I've never seen before
Snickers played because he loved me
Flash loved the sport more than anything
When I became homeless I had no choice but to give him
to my trainer
I believed she would continue to compete with him
If I couldn't be with him
I thought I could at least give him
The game
He loved to work
In a way that rivals the commitment of Sirius

Rally is Sirius' sport of choice unless you put her in front
of water
This summer I watched her come to life
Bumper buoy in mouth
Retrieve
Retrieve
Conquering nervous fear of waves

That kept her from
The sea some high tide days last summer when she was
only a baby

Retrieve
Dog mouth wrapped around neon orange floating plastic
bumper
Retrieve
Retrieve
Bringing me back memories of watching a dog work
Something spiritual
Genetics kick in as she does the
Work
She's bred to do
Her purpose
Retrieve
Retrieve
Memories of ancestors you've never known.
Dogs who jumped from boats to save lives
Who crossed the continent to deliver
Manifest density
Colonialistic flawed but Seaman was an incredible dog
Rigel the dog who swam in the icy water as the Titanic
sank
To rescue lifeboat number 4
When the fog hid it from
The rescuers
It was Rigel, a dog whose bark brought light and boats and
life to those on board
Eventually heaved on board the rescue ship
His master drowned
He had saved so many but
His First Officer
Went down with the ship (and so many others who never
made it into lifeboats)
There was to be a dog show on the Titanic
A show that never was

Healing/Heeling

So many of the dogs drowning in the kennels
But Rigel was free and swam

Seaman led Lewis and Clark west to Oregon
Sirius in her own way is leading me west
I am
So afraid of the anxiety that has
So many times
Ruled my life
Service dog at my side
Alert
Alerting

I am never more passionate than when I am working with
a dog
And never more afraid
Dogs are my greatest passion
And my greatest fear
I never measure up
I am
Never good enough for them
I never see myself as deserving of them

This is flawed
It is the unhealthy anxiety voice calling
Will I ever be good enough for the dogs
Will I ever know enough
Be consistent enough

I worry worry worry
That I've done everything wrong somehow
And then as I lay here writing
Phone under blankets
Pre dawn
In the Iowa truck stop
The largest in the world
Charlotte watches the trucks pull into the truck wash

Tail wagging
My partner
Who talked me down
Who patiently listens to my insecurity and panic
Sleeps before another day of driving

My foot slips from under the blankets and Sirius licks it
Drool lips
Warm tongue
Cold nose
I am enough for her
I am enough for the dogs I share my life with
I am enough for my partner and the family we have built
I am enough
I am enough
I am enough for my dogs
I have trained them well
They are not robots
They are not perfect
They come with their own histories and fears and
insecurities
They come with their own passions
There is no rule book to life
This is not a carefully choreographed sport
I am enough for them
Will I ever be enough for myself?

The hardest thing to learn to do in any dog sport is to trust
the dog
When the dog understands the game
When you have trained each aspect
At that point
the hardest thing
Is to trust your dog
Trust your dog
In Dog I trust

Someday perhaps I will develop reasonable expectations
(of myself)
Someday perhaps I will trust myself
When I hold a leash

LETTING GO

When I leave you at the clinic for surgery I am overcome
with the memory of the leashes I
Let go
The leashes that were ripped from my hands
I center my breathing
Do the things the dogs have taught me to do
To
Cue calm
I focus on the memory of you in your passion
Swim
Retrieve
Swim
Retrieve
Swim
Retrieve

Orange bumper floating in the Atlantic waves off the tip
of Cape Cod.

Swim
Retrieve
Swim
Retrieve
Swim
Retrieve

SEARCH

Nose Work is a sport the civilian equivalent of the search/rescue, narcotics, bomb sniffing, and cadaver work that police and military dogs do. In this case, dogs are searching boxes for a specific odor (birch, anise, or clove), which they need to alert the handler to. At early stages of the game, the target scent is paired with primary odor (food).

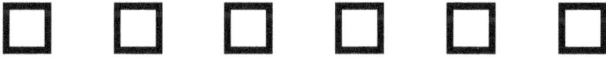

□ □ □ □ □ □

Search.
I am more anxious than i have ever been
No
Not ever
Not more anxious than
When I was
alone
But very
Anxious
More anxious than I have been in years
Or maybe I am just saying that aloud
Maybe it is the moving, the return to a place that was
mostly one of fear

Trust your dog
Search
I am searching to be less anxious
I am saying the words PTSD again
Naming
Claiming
Waking clutching

My retired service dog's leash
Remembering how he
Guided
Me toward building this life

I am always
Anxious
I don't like to admit
Weakness
Trauma is not weakness (I say in my writing)
If only I could always believe that about myself

Memories of field, early morning, long line,
Turkey legs
Dragged
Dew
Frost
Dogs pulling at harness
Leash in hand
Search

That was then
Now we search odor in boxes
Watching pricked ears
My most anxious dog coming alive with drive
Pulsing nose

□   □   □

□   □   □

□

Search
Quiet.
The hardest part of this sport is
                    Quiet.
Not crowding my dog with chatter
Silencing my mind
I'm not good at quiet
The anxiety voice is loud
So loud
But I quiet it to watch

As her greying muzzle puzzles through boxes
Trusting my dog.
Trusting myself
Our collective traumas (for once) silent

Search

When did you become an old dog
It hits me
That you had a life before the life we have built together

Healing/Heeling

One you probably (I hope) don't remember
A life without carpet and toys and vacations and
mountains, beach wanders, wading, birthday cakes, car
rides
One of my greatest joys has been building a big (safe)
world for you
One in stark contrast to the streets where you came
But it means I am
Uncertain
If you are
Eight
Or nine
Or
Ten
But probably not eleven

I see the grey creep across your muzzle
Under your paws
The stiffness to your step
But you
Always come running the moment I whisper your name
From across the house
No matter how deeply you sleep you
Always
Come to me
Come for me
Explore any dark room
Any strange noise
Now with the best recall of any of my dogs

You understand the way trauma can pause a moment
The way panic can overtake a day
You started your life
We don't know where
You lived on the streets
My body shakes with fear when I think of what your life
must have been back then

Not knowing where your meals would come from

You charm most everyone who meets you
Except stranger dogs - your greatest enemy
The nose that kept you alive
That found food for your puppies
For yourself
That found safe places to sleep
Is now twitching with pleasure
Honed
Ready
To find odor
Search
Search
Search

RALLY RETURN

*
*
*
*
SERPENTINE
WEAVE TWICE

HALT   DOG SPINS
HALT
TURN RIGHT   RIGHT   STEP
IN
1 STEP   FORWARD
FRONT
CALL TO HEEL   FINISH
RIGHT

                       FORWARD

                   RIGHT TURN

HALT   MOVING SIDESTEP RIGHT
1 STEP
2 STEPS
3 STEPS

270° LEFT   HALT WALK AROUND [ ]   START

FINISH

START
The surgeon says that your joints have been
"Remodeled"
They show me x-ray images
Bone
Healed
The physical therapist says the only thing holding you back now is my
Fear
(What else is new)
That you are ready
To return to normal activity
Running with your sister
Hikes
The swim specialist says your swimming is
Strong
Collected
You are cleared for swimming outside the rehab pool

BROAD JUMP
I hold my breath
You don't break
Just like the surgeon said you wouldn't

HALT WALK AROUND
I send the entry fee for your first trial

270 LEFT
It isn't about the competition
It's the dance that brings me back

HALT 1 STEP 2 STEPS 3 STEPS
To be looked at the way you look at me
Almost
Absolves me of the guilt I feel for all those years ago
failing to be an adult
And not being able to provide my dogs a home at
seventeen
When I became homeless

HALT TURN RIGHT 1 STEP CALL TO HEEL
I hold myself to impossibly high standards

DOG SPINS RIGHT FORWARD
Dogs remind me daily
Of forgiveness

HALT STEP IN FRONT FINISH RIGHT
FORWARD
RIGHT TURN
SERPENTINE WEAVE TWICE
MOVING SIDESTEP RIGHT

I tell my partner over dinner that when this book is
published
When I have confessed all my dog stories
When I have immortalized their lives
I might be ready to forgive
Myself

FINISH

HALT STEP IN FRONT
FINISH LEFT
FORWARD

RIGHT TURN

RIGHT TURN   FIGURE 8 NO DISTRACTIONS

      *   *

CALL FRONT
RETURN TO
HEEL

SERPENTINE
WEAVE ONCE

HALT, CALL FRONT
FINISH RIGHT   *
FORWARD

*

HALT DOG CIRCLES RIGHT
SIT

*

*

270° RIGHT   HALT 1 STEP, 2 STEPS, 3 STEPS

START

ROSE CITY CLASSIC

I dreamed of dog shows the way that other children fantasized about amusement parks (it wasn't until adulthood that I gained my own love of those): Westminster, Crufts, Rose City Classic. These shows are not of the same caliber, but to a dog obsessed pre-internet kid growing up in Oregon, they were. Crufts and Westminster I read about in magazines or watched on TV. Every year I would go to Rose City, dragging a bored parent through the aisles of vendors, sitting transfixed by the breed rings, then later the sporting events. Cutting the newsprint ads for the show out of the newspaper and plastering them on my bedroom wall, on my school notebooks

START   *   *   RIGHT TURN
         *

OFFSET SERPENTINE RIGHT

270 LEFT   RIGHT TURN

                          FAST

PACE

FRONT
1 BACK   360 RIGHT
2 BACK
3 BACK   MOVING SIDE STEP
RIGHT

FINISH

270 RIGHT

NORMAL PACE

HALT	HALT	CALL FRONT
270		
RIGHT	WALK	FINISH LEFT
LEFT		
FORWARD	ABOUT	FORWARD

Though it was only one dog of mine who entered the ring, all three brought me to this moment and the ghosts of others heeled beside me when the judge asked if I was ready.

Sirius stood by my side, heeled and then, as we neared the end of the course rolled on the ring mats, catching a whiff of…..something delicious. Tail wagging. Goofy grin. The judge wasn't amused, but I was. I remembered Snickers' first agility trial how he woo woo woooed at the judge and ran his own course. I laughed. We finished the course having fun - something more important than any ribbon.

Dogs have made me, and saved me, and remind me daily to never take myself too seriously.

The pain was worth it to have the chance for this dance.

ACKNOWLEDGEMENTS

Thank you first and foremost to all the dogs who have made me, and saved me: Peepers, Snickers, Flash, Sydney, Cosmo, Mercury, Charlotte and Sirius. Without you, I would be nothing – may this book in some small way do justice to who you are and what you have meant to me.

Thank you to my queer dog friends: my good friend and mentor Frankie Joiris and my goddoghter Kiss~Me. Thank you to Holly Hughes and Esther Newton for showing me that a world of queer dog people existed. Thank you to Michael Thomas Ford for sharing my love of dog stories. Thank you to Emma Arlington M for reading early drafts of this book and confirming I really could write hybrid. Thank you to Michael Klein for workshopping part of this book in his Master Class in Hybrid at Goddard College in Vermont. Thank you to all of the dog people who have shaped my life and journey in dog worlds including all the trainers I've worked with over the years.

Most of all, thank you to my partner Kestryl, who might not have always identified as "a dog person" but who is the best dog co-parent I could have ever dreamed of. Ze is as obsessed with our pack as I am, and who selflessly volunteers to spend evenings and weekends taking the dogs on adventures, training classes, and dog shows. The dogs and I are so lucky to have you.

ABOUT THE AUTHOR

Sassafras Lowrey is a teenage runaway who grew up to become the 2013 winner of the Lambda Literary Emerging Writer Award. Hir books have been honored by organizations ranging from the National Leather Association to the American Library Association.

Sassafras has been involved with dog sports and dog training for over twenty years from Competition Obedience, Dog Agility, Tricks, Rally Obedience, Parkour and more. Sassafras is a Certified Trick Dog Instructor (CTDI) and has achieved the honor of Trainer of the Year from Do More With Your Dog the first official trick dog titling organization. Sassafras' dogs have achieved Champion Trick Dog (the highest level of trick competition), and Trick Dog Performer titles. Sassafras has written regularly for leading local and national dog magazines for over a decade.
www.SassafrasLowrey.com

Also by Sassafras Lowrey:

Lost Boi

Roving Pack

A Little Queermas Carol

Leather Ever After

Kicked Out

TRICKS IN THE CITY: For Daring Dogs And The
Humans That Love Them

Bedtime Stories For Rescue Dogs

www.ingramcontent.com/pod-product-compliance
Lightning Source LLC
Chambersburg PA
CBHW021934040426

42448CB00008B/1060